ALAIN PROUST: A PORTRAIT OF CAPE TOWN

FERNWOOD PRESS
P O BOX 15344
VLAEBERG 8018

REGISTRATION NUMBER 90/04463/07

FIRST PUBLISHED 1994

COPYRIGHT © PHOTOGRAPHS ALAIN PROUST, 1994
COPYRIGHT © TEXT PETER BORCHERT, 1994
COPYRIGHT © ILLUSTRATIONS SIMON BARLOW, 1994
COPYRIGHT © SATELLITE PHOTOGRAPH ON PAGE 6 SATELLITE
APPLICATIONS CENTRE, MIKONTEC, CSIR, PRETORIA

DESIGN BY WILLEM JORDAAN, CAPE TOWN
EDITING BY LENI MARTIN, CAPE TOWN
PRODUCTION CONTROL BY ABDUL LATIEF (BUNNY) GALLIE, CAPE TOWN
TYPESETTING BY DIATYPE SETTING CC, CAPE TOWN
REPRODUCTION BY UNIFOTO (PTY) LTD, CAPE TOWN
PRINTED AND BOUND BY TIEN WAH PRESS (PTE) LTD, SINGAPORE

ISBN 1 874950 09 1

FERNWOOD
PRESS

Table Mountain from the Delheim wine estate just outside Stellenbosch, some 50 kilometres east of the city.

ALAIN PROUST A PORTRAIT OF CAPE TOWN

TEXT BY PETER BORCHERT

*To my wife Mary,
and our sons Nicolas
and Jacques*

Alain Proust.

Sunshine protea.

After 21 years of living here it seems a little strange to admit that I came to Cape Town by accident. But that is how it happened. My intention had been to leave France and go to work in Australia, but while waiting for my papers to come through I accepted a friend's invitation to join him on a visit to Cape Town. I knew nothing of South Africa other than apartheid and that every so often we played rugby against one another.

Having been met at Jan Smuts airport in Johannesburg, we were whisked off into the night, heading for Cape Town. We arrived in Welkom in the early hours of the morning. To find ourselves in a Free State mining town early on a Sunday, only 36 hours after leaving Paris, was something of a culture shock. We resumed our journey and by the middle of the following afternoon were climbing Du Toit's Kloof. It was a clear November afternoon when we reached the top of the pass, and I will never forget that first magnificent view of Table Mountain, still some 60 kilometres away.

Settling in was easy, and through a friend who worked at the National Gallery we soon had the occasional assignment to photograph some of the gallery's exhibits. This led to being commissioned by Pieter Struik to take the photographs for a series of books on South African artists. Most of my work has been studio photography for advertising and publishing, but in my spare time I have always carried a camera to record the changing moods of the city. A book on Cape Town became a logical step.

The view southwards from Blouberg – Table Mountain with Devil's Peak (left) and Lion's Head (right).

Sour fig.

It is difficult not to make political statements in one's work, however inadvertently, but I have tried to avoid doing so. I am aware that in presenting my *Portrait of Cape Town* I have left myself open to criticism that some things have been included and others left out. What I have set out to portray are those aspects and elements of the city that appeal to my aesthetic sense. I love the mountain and its environment, I love the crisp light of early morning and the warm light of evening. I like the different seasons and the moods of the sea and sky. I find little appeal in Cape Town's contemporary buildings, but I enjoy the architecture of the past. I am constantly overwhelmed by the grandeur of the setting.

In trying to capture all this on film I have taken thousands of photographs, and in the task of selecting a mere 400 for this book I have been influenced and guided by publisher Pieter Struik and designer Willem Jordaan. Thus they have helped to determine the final shape of the book. I am grateful to them both, and particularly to Pieter who, with drive and determination, ensured that my vision could find expression in these pages.

I would also like to express my gratitude to my wife Mary for sharing with me her knowledge and love of Cape Town; to my sons for patiently giving up their weekends so that we could go out and photograph; and to my colleague Dick Bomford for his encouragement and support.

Cape Town and its people have been good to me, and this book is my tribute to a city that has both spiritually and physically become my home.

ROBBEN ISLAND

TABLE BAY

CAPE TOWN

SEA POINT

CLIFTON

CAMPS BAY

LLANDUDNO

HOUT BAY

STRANDFONTEIN

MUIZENBERG

ST JAMES

NOORDHOEK

KALK BAY

FISH HOEK

KOMMETJIE

GLENCAIRN

SIMON'S TOWN

FALSE BAY

SMITSWINKEL BAY

ATLANTIC OCEAN

CAPE POINT

CAPE OF GOOD HOPE

This satellite photograph shows the Cape
Peninsula and part of the Cape Flats. The
dark, textured colouring represents mountain
areas; the dark red dense natural vegetation
shades to the lighter urban vegetation; the
light blue denotes urban development; and
the solid black areas are water bodies.

The Cape Peninsula

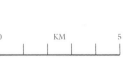

N

0   KM   5

From the top of the Tygerberg, looking out over the northern suburbs of Cape Town.

INTRODUCTION

Sugarbush.

At the southern tip of the continent a thin, gnarled finger of land projects defiantly from mainland Africa into the sea, challenging the might of the Atlantic Ocean that all but surrounds it. Sculpted by time and the elements, this peninsula is a place of great beauty, dominated by an imposing mountainous spine that in places drops sheer into the sea. At its northern limit the mountain chain terminates triumphantly in the Table Mountain massif which, with its two cohorts of Lion's Head and Devil's Peak, forms the backdrop to Cape Town, Africa's most southerly city and the home of some four million people.

Table Mountain and its attendant peaks dominate the landscape. No matter what the approach – by land, sea or air – it is there, looming in the distance like an island, its feet shrouded in haze and sometimes fog. For centuries it has been the landfall of mariners, from those that sailed in the puny caravels of the Portuguese, and maybe before that, to the era of the Dutch and English merchantmen. It has witnessed the arrival of the first steamships, the coming and passing of the regular-as-clockwork mailboat service, and it has watched huge supertankers labouring through the swell far to the south, as well as yachtsmen facing the challenge of its notorious off-shore waters for sport.

Usually the mountain presides benignly over its narrow coastal plain and the waters beyond, but at times it presents the face of fury itself. Then, lashed by the fearful windstorms that can approach out of nowhere no matter what the season, the rocky headlands and shoals lie waiting

The northern face of Table Mountain
from near Durbanville . . .

Red Afrikaner.

to dash the unlucky, the unwary and those foolish enough to treat the Cape of Storms with scant respect.

The weather, in fact, is a subject that dominates the passing conversation of Capetonians, demanding our attention and conditioning our daily lives throughout the year. A long while ago, a fellow Capetonian who has written much about the culture of the Cape Peninsula and its surrounds spoke with wry humour of this extraordinary place so 'delicately poised between the tropics and the Antarctic'.

Anyone who has spent any length of time in Cape Town will immediately understand what he meant, for few places on earth can possibly match it for sudden and often dramatic changes in the weather. In summer, particularly during the months of December, January and March, strong winds drive in from the southeast. Sometimes for weeks on end they nag and buffet, whining and whistling through the city and moaning across the flat isthmus that joins the Peninsula to its hinterland. It is a dry time of the year and the Southeaster makes it more so, greedily sucking the moisture from the land and the humour from its inhabitants. But then, suddenly, it will drop and a stillness settles on the city. At first the sense of relief is palpable, but it may not last, for without the cooling effect of the wind the temperature often soars into the upper thirties and the city and its inhabitants sweat, soon wishing for the return of the Cape Doctor to blow away the heat and the thick smog that can lie like a shroud over the land.

By contrast, it has been known to snow on Table Mountain – not often and never lasting, but snow none the less. More characteristically, the Cape winters are simply damp, with wave after wave of cold fronts marching like armies across the southern oceans to throw themselves in full frontal attack against the ramparts of the mountain. The squalls are often frightening in their ferocity and they can cause serious damage and hardship. In a moment trees can be uprooted, watercourses that are dry for nine months of the year become raging torrents. And when the clouds draw back momentarily it is as if the curtain has suddenly gone up on some classical Andean scene – the granite cliffs of the mountain glisten and water cascades in falls of a hundred metres or more.

. . . and from Signal Hill.

It is of course these legendary summer and winter storms that make Cape Town the butt of banter from upcountry dwellers who flaunt their more equable and predictable weather cycles. But the true Capetonian revels in the ever-changing moods. The storms have a magnificence and power that can be exhilarating and they provide a counterpoint for those balmy times in between, usually in spring and autumn, when a soft, gentle light bathes the Cape and the air has a crispness and sparkle to it; then Cape Town is the most beautiful place on earth.

No-one knows for sure when man first came to the Cape, but undoubtedly it was a long time ago. Shellfish middens along the coast have been carbon dated at some 100 000 years before the present, while archaeological evidence gleaned from Peers Cave in the sandstone ridge of mountains above Fish Hoek suggests a culture moving towards the Middle Stone Age around 35 000 years ago. Other sites along the coast seem to corroborate these findings, but the record is frustratingly incomplete and likely to remain so, for the time coincided closely with the low sea level of the last glaciation and it could well be that most of the sites now lie hidden beneath the turbulent waters of the western Cape's bays and coves.

At some stage between then and the arrival of Europeans at the southern tip of Africa, communities of yellow-skinned herders established themselves at the Cape. How and when they first arrived are also questions that are unlikely to be satisfactorily answered, but these were the indigenous people with whom European explorers first came into contact at the end of the fifteenth century. Time and the people and cultures of northern Europe were not kind to the ways of these small, gracile pastoralists and inexorably they were moved into oblivion. Now little remains to remind us of the existence of these Khoisan (a collective term now widely used in place of the words Bushmen and Hottentot which have pejorative connotations), save in their physical attributes which persist to an extent in the appearance of some Capetonians of mixed descent.

It is possible – and some sources contend – that Arabian, Indian, Chinese or even Phoenician merchants were the first seamen to round Cape Point, but the course of uninterrupted recorded history begins with the Portuguese. As has so often been the case in the exploration of the world, their motivation was trade. Overland access to the marketplaces of the Orient was difficult at the best

A row of stately stone pines . . .

Kalkoentjie.

of times and became even more so with the spread of Islam through the Middle East, North Africa and into southern Europe. Spurred on by the need for an alternative route, it was during the reign of João II that Bartholomeu Dias embarked on his quest to find a way to India by way of the southern tip of the African continent. By default he did round the Cape, as without at first realizing it he was literally blown around it during what must have been a terrifying storm. He made landfall at the present-day Mossel Bay some 200 kilometres to the east of Cape Point, but he was not to achieve his passage to India, for soon afterwards he was 'persuaded' by a mutinous crew to head for home. Although it was his compatriot, Vasco da Gama, who a few years later did open the sea route to Goa, the Portuguese did not lay any claim to the Cape, favouring instead havens on the west and east coasts of Africa as their revictualling stations. It fell to the Dutch, who had become highly successful competitors in the lucrative trade with the East, to establish a permanent settlement at the foot of Table Mountain.

For generations, South African schoolchildren have been instructed that our country's story began in 1652 with the landing in Table Bay of the Dutch commander, Jan van Riebeeck, and his small company of men. Thankfully this patently untrue and gross presumption is being supplanted in the minds of young people by a broader and more accurate perspective, but the seminal influence of the Dutch on the Cape and indeed the whole of South Africa cannot be denied. Their rule of the Cape, though stutteringly begun through early attempts at agriculture in defiance of an unpredictable and often malign climate, slowly took hold and, once securely rooted, began to flourish. For a century and a half the will of Holland held sway at the Cape. The tiny settlement with its wood-and-mud fort and meagre buildings began to grow into a town of some size, with

. . . lines the road to the
Signal Hill lookout point.

imposing edifices, wide dusty streets, noisome canals and an impressive five-bastioned castle
complete with moat. During this period farms were established in what are now the suburbs of
the city, vines were planted and slaves imported.

The Dutch had little regard for the indigenous Khoisan people and viewed them as unsuitable
for labour. Instead they brought in slaves, first from other parts of Africa and subsequently
from the East. It was these newcomers from the Dutch East India Company's far-flung colonial
possessions who were the forebears of the people now known as the Cape Malays, a strongly
cohesive Muslim community that has contributed hugely to Cape Town and its uniquely cosmopolitan character. Ironically, however, very few 'Malays' actually came from Malaysia; most came
from Java and elsewhere in Indonesia.

And then came the British. Their first arrival was tentative and short-lived, but in 1806 an
expeditionary force landed at Blaauwberg on the northern shores of Table Bay with a vengeance.
The battle was short and decisive, and soon the Union Jack fluttered from the seat of government, continuing to do so for the next 150 years. The British way became indelibly engraved on
life and society at the Cape; industry and commerce grew in stature and with it an emergent Cape
Town began to spread its wings. More imposing buildings, now reflecting the influences and
styles of the Empire, began to raise their turrets, domes and spires above the skyline. The ornate
and often elaborate façades of the Victorian and Edwardian period jostled side by side with the
sterner, plainer lines of Dutch architecture, and English street names – Darling, Adderley, Queen
Victoria – began to vie with Buitenkant, Buitengracht, Bree and Waterkant. The harbour grew in
tandem with the British merchant fleet, and Cape Town basked in a maritime importance to
match that of Singapore, Hong Kong, Sydney, Calcutta and the other far-flung ports of the

Cloud patterns over Lion's Head, an indication of Cape Town's changeable weather.

Mimetes. colonies. The tentacles of imperialism stretching from Government House into Africa were not always greeted with enthusiasm by those already occupying the land. Bitter border struggles ensued with indigenous people to the east and in the north, where long-disgruntled Dutch-speaking pioneer farmers had trekked to establish their own promised land, antipathy towards the Cape government erupted into hostility and war, spurred on by the discovery of gold and diamonds.

Cape Town, always the springboard for these ambitions and adventures into the interior, remained largely aloof and untouched by the attrition and hardship on the periphery of its control. The city, aside from the bawdy, rough life of the harbour taverns and the rude dwellings of its less prosperous inhabitants, was a place of high society, with banquets and balls in the homes of note, horse racing on the common and elegant carriage rides down oak- and plane-lined avenues. Many of the affluent Dutch families who did not feel moved to join with their pioneering compatriots were absorbed into the colonial society, and in the process many became more British than the British themselves.

But it wasn't all frivolity, for during the same period the Cape was moving slowly but surely towards independent government. The foundation of an economic infrastructure of banks and insurance societies was being laid; hospitals were established, as were schools and seats of higher learning. Cape Town, too, became a focus of the scientific world. Dilettante botanists and natural historians came to collect specimens and to wonder over the evolutionary miracle of the Cape flora.

Such intrigue with the natural world was the order of the day, the age of enquiry and enlightenment. At the Cape, however, it found added expression, for here on this tiny peninsula at the end of the world more than 2 600 species of plants have been identified to date, far more than in the whole of the British Isles. Some, such as the beautiful silver tree and the inappropriately named Guernsey lily, occur here and nowhere else. Table Mountain itself has more than 1 400 indigenous species and it is little wonder that it is a national monument and is awaiting declaration as a world heritage site. But it is not for aesthetic reasons alone that the mountain chain of the peninsula is treasured; there are sound social and economic reasons as well. It is

undoubtedly one of the landmarks of the world and has huge recreational and ecotourism value. If wisely managed it has the potential to earn substantial revenue for Cape Town and its citizens. Furthermore, the vegetation that is so intriguing and wonderful has evolved with the terrain itself; it has adapted to the harsh living on poor soils and to survive the fires that ravage the mountain from time to time. Also, and probably most important of all, the natural vegetation maximizes the amount of water that reaches streams, and in conjunction with the sandstone substrata, is a vital aquifer for the supply of clean water for the benefit of all.

It is such environmental issues that face the Cape Town of today. It has passed through the Dutch and British stages of its development. It has witnessed and played a huge role in the country's progress through the twentieth century. It has survived the 'development years' when much of its modern face appeared, with scant and sometimes no attention at all being given to aesthetics – for example, the development of an architecturally barren Foreshore on reclaimed ground, a monstrosity that separated Cape Town from the waterfront with which it had grown up. It has survived the 'apartheid years' during which people who had for centuries been an integral part of the city and had the birthright to be there, were forcibly moved to the sand-blown flats beyond the city limits. The hurt and harm remain, the scar of District Six is still there, but now there is a sense of healing.

There is a feeling of community that is bringing its inhabitants together again with a sense of common purpose to tackle the environmental and social problems that derive from Cape Town being one of the fastest-growing conurbations in the world. There is a sense of opportunity, too; people want to see their city succeed, to offer it as an Olympic venue with pride.

In world terms Cape Town is a young city, a mere three and a half centuries into its life, but it is the oldest city in southern Africa and as such is steeped in the history of the land and its people. At almost every turn there is something – a cobbled street, perhaps, or some Victorian ironwork, a Cape Dutch façade, or maybe a stately old tree – to remind one of a bygone era. But it is a modern city as well, filled with vibrancy, enthusiasm and confidence in its future.

Few people would argue with Cape Town's claim to be one of the loveliest cities in the world. It seems to have everything – mountains, forests, beautiful beaches, winelands and some of the finest architecture in the land. But it has more than just physical beauty: it has a soul.

Two views of Cape Town from Signal Hill.

Central Cape Town is not very big – its business district, with a skyline dominated by moderately high-rise office towers, has an area of little more than a square kilometre. At its rear, the inner city suburbs encroach inland, but their advance is soon thwarted by planning regulations and the steep rise of Table Mountain, Devil's Peak, Lion's Head and Signal Hill. Seawards it is the ocean that limits development, even though the natural contour of Table Bay has been somewhat altered by the development of Duncan Dock, Cape Town's main harbour, which began in 1938. In the process some 194 hectares were reclaimed from the sea, giving the city its Foreshore which, although now built on and bisected by highways, remains apart, for most a soulless intrusion that has never been successfully integrated with the Mother City. To the west and southwards Cape Town manages to squeeze past the headland of Signal Hill, continuing in a thin ribbon of urban and suburban development along the Atlantic coast. To the north and east, however, it escapes via a wider passage between land and sea. This is where the real sprawl of greater Cape Town begins – like the floodwaters of a storm, people and their dwellings spread out over the flat, sandy isthmus that joins Cape Town to its hinterland.

The Waterfront, where Cape Town and Capetonians are being reunited with the city's dockland.

For more than 20 years Cape Town was effectively separated from its waterfront by the Foreshore reclamation which placed hundreds of thousands of tonnes of landfill between the city and its harbour – a sad and ironic fate for a port long known throughout the maritime world as 'the Tavern of the Seas'. Happily, all bad things come to an end and in the early 1990s a bold scheme began to take shape, inspired by other contemporary dockland redevelopments as far afield as Sydney, London and Los Angeles. Around the old harbour – the Alfred Basin where sailing ships formerly moored and the adjacent Victoria Dock – old sheds, warehouses and harbour buildings of historical and architectural note were carefully stripped and then, with sensitivity and imagination, refashioned into new life. Already 'The Waterfront' has refocused Cape Town's leisure and entertainment attention, although only the initial phases of the project have been completed.

1 The lofty interior of the V&A shopping mall.
2 The eastern façade of the shopping complex.
3 'Quay Four', popular restaurant and watering hole.
4 Aerial view of the Waterfront.
5 The west entrance to the V&A mall.

Dock Road Theatre and Café.

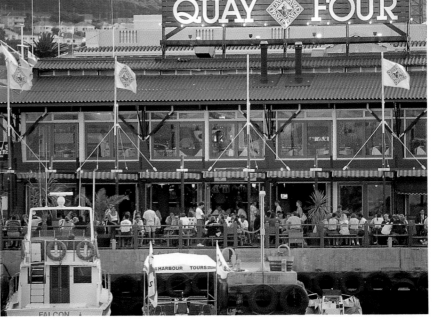

1 2
5 4
3

The retail hub of the Waterfront is the huge Victoria and Alfred (V&A) shopping complex – virtually a city within a city, where supermarkets, bookstores and cinemas rub shoulders with clothing boutiques, African art and curio galleries, and other speciality shops and stalls. Eating (and drinking), however, is the major activity at the Waterfront, with restaurants and pubs catering to all tastes and pockets from haute cuisine and ethnic through to steakhouses, coffee shops, ice-cream parlours and open-air food stalls. Busking and street theatre add to the Waterfront's weekend carnival atmosphere, but as the day wears on, especially on Sunday evenings, the entertainment moves under cover, the rhythms of jazz escaping through the windows and doors of many a night spot. One such venue is the Green Dolphin in the shopping mall of the Victoria and Alfred Hotel – the long white building towards the bottom right-hand corner of the aerial photograph opposite. The hotel, which boasts a Waterfront Café and Terrace overlooking the Alfred Basin and an uninterrupted view of Table Mountain, is a fine example of the architect's skill in converting a dilapidated warehouse into luxury accommodation.

1 Stripping the paint from the hull of a Taiwanese trawler.
2 A pilot boat bustles towards its charge.
3 The container terminal.

The Waterfront development lies primarily along the eastern flank of the Alfred and Victoria basins, whence it gets its name. Although the piers and quays are being given over to entertainment, the old harbour still works for its living, with fishing and other craft constantly on the move. The principal commercial life of Cape Town's harbour, however, lies to the west in the Duncan Dock, which was opened in 1943, and in the huge container and bulk handling terminal. Once the graceful mailships of the Union-Castle Line and other shipping companies were regular visitors to the Duncan Dock but, apart from a few visiting pleasure cruisers, the days of the passenger liners are sadly past. Never in recent times has Cape Town been South Africa's busiest

1

2

3

1 A long lens makes city and mountain loom deceptively close behind fishing vessels in the harbour.
2 The harbour complex, the container harbour and tanker terminal in the foreground and Duncan Dock behind.
3 Paarden Eiland, a light industrial area west of the harbour.

port – that status belongs to Durban which alone accounts for some 50 per cent of the country's sea freight. Nevertheless, handling cargo and the servicing of ships reached its peak in Cape Town when hostilities in the Middle East forced the closure of the Suez Canal during the 1960s. Now the harbour works well below its capacity and for the most part it is a bleak and windswept place, uninviting aside from the haven of the Royal Cape Yacht Club tucked into a small corner and nearby Panama Jack's, an unpretentious restaurant that has won renown for its seafood – it is one of the few eateries in Cape Town where both west and east coast crayfish of prodigious size are regularly on the menu.

2

3

1 The 'Malay Quarter' on
the slopes of Signal Hill.
2 Looking towards Kloof
Nek, the saddle between Table
Mountain and Lion's Head.
3 Lion's Head and Signal Hill
seen from the cableway.

Contrasts are a feature of Cape Town, particularly in its architecture and culture. Some areas, such as Schotsche Kloof
in the Malay Quarter, may appear somewhat dilapidated and insalubrious, but the buildings have an integrity and are part of
a cohesive community, unlike the blight of the three apartment towers comprising the Disa Park complex on the far side of the city. Since
their erection in the 1970s they have offended the sensibilities of Capetonians and visitors alike – a visual degradation of an aspirant
world heritage site. Below the towers and to the right, where the low saddle of Kloof Nek allows access to the Atlantic seaboard, the steep,
tree-lined streets are more discreet and the intrusion of man up a mountainside once wooded with indigenous silver trees is softened
with some fine architecture, both contemporary and of the past. Any reservations about Cape Town's architecture are, however, soon
forgotten as one is borne up Table Mountain in a cable car, and the magnificence of the city and its setting unfolds below.

Mount Nelson Hotel – luxury suites . . .

Downtown high-rise.

The noon-day gun.

Waterkant Street.

. . . and a view through the garden.

Pediment of the National Gallery.

Laughing dove.

While some of Cape Town's high-rise buildings may have individual merit, most are functional with little to set them apart from those that crowd the central business district of any modern city. Only glimpses of the mountain behind place them without doubt. The grace and charm of the 'Mother City' come from bygone, colonial times and can be seen in the simplicity of the homes of the 'Bokaap' or so-called Malay Quarter, redolent of English Regency, or in the sophisticated elegance of the Mount Nelson Hotel. One of the oldest structures in Cape Town is 'The Castle', or more correctly, The Castle of Good Hope. The cornerstone was laid in 1666 and for the next 13 years timber was dragged from Hout Bay, stone was shipped from Robben Island quarries and lime from shells was burnt on the beaches to construct what has been a symbol of military authority ever since. Over the centuries it has been added to and altered, but the original five-bastioned design remains. At the other end of the city, above Parliament, is the Mount Nelson Hotel. The 'Nellie', as the hotel is affectionately known, opened its doors in March 1899 at the zenith of the British Empire and to much fanfare. With its distinctive pink coat, it has now held its position as one of the world's most renowned hotels for nearly a century.

The Castle of Good Hope.

Upper Strand Street.

District Six.

The Lutheran Church, Strand Street.

The Lutheran Church, with its Gothic and classical detailing, owes its existence to Martin Melck, a prosperous farmer of the late eighteenth century and a leader in the small but growing Lutheran community. In 1771 Melck gave his fellow worshippers permission to hold services in his barn on Strand Street. A few years later, with the advent of greater religious tolerance, the barn was converted into a church, its façade designed by Anton Anreith, one of the country's most renowned architects. To the east of the church Melck set aside land for a parsonage which was completed only after his death. Known as Martin Melck House, it was also designed by Anreith and is regarded as a particularly fine example of a townhouse of the period. To the left of the church is the sexton's house, now restored and in use as the Netherlands Embassy.

Bree Street.

1 Cultural History Museum, Church Square.
2 Corporation Street.
3 Waterkant Street.
4 Adderley Street.

The Standard Bank, Adderley Street.

Lower Burg Street.

Detail from the City Hall.

The City Hall.

Redwinged Starling.

In many of the city's central streets contemporary office blocks crowd tightly together as they compete for the sky, but here and there a grand old lady presides, pushing pretenders to the side and creating light and space. In Adderley Street, the Standard Bank building first rose above the city in 1880. It was heightened during the 1920s, but the central dome with its figure of Britannia remained to remind the city of Victoria and the Empire. The façade of the bank is graced by a classical portico of impressive proportion that stands a full two storeys above the street. Inside, the architecture of the banking hall has been compromised by the demands of a modern financial institution, but the rich mahogany tellers' booths and the lofty columns bearing an ornate ceiling remain. Around the corner, in Darling Street, is the City Hall, a majestic building in the Italian Renaissance style. It is of later vintage than the Standard Bank, the foundation stone having been laid only in 1900 and the building completed in 1905. Ironically, the city had no civic focus until this time, although the suburbs already had long-established municipalities, each with its own town hall. The administration of Cape Town has moved to a soulless slab on the Foreshore, but the City Hall remains well used – the Cape Town Symphony Orchestra has its home there and every Thursday and Sunday evenings loyal supporters gather in the grand hall with its magnificent Norman Beard organ for their weekly injection of classical music.

Entrance to the South African Museum.

Elaborate ironwork – whether purely decorative or also functional – is a hallmark of the Victorian period.

It has been said that the South African Museum, with its peculiarly Republican style, could well have stood on Church Square in Pretoria instead of at the top end of the Gardens above Parliament in Cape Town. Not surprisingly, perhaps, for the man who designed it in 1893 happened to be the government architect of the Boer Republic of the Orange Free State. The interior of the building has been much altered over the years, although the majestic main staircase remains. Among the museum's many attractions is the Whale Room where the full skeleton of a blue whale hangs in the vault-like chamber, seeming to glide peacefully through the subdued light. The Whale Room, renowned for its acoustics, is the venue of many music recitals. A San display in another part of the museum depicts aspects of the culture of these early inhabitants of southern Africa, including their world-famous rock art. Adjacent to the museum in Queen Victoria Street is the Planetarium, under the auspices of which popular lectures and courses on the wonders of the southern skies are held.

Courtyard, Martin Melck House.

Somerset Hospital.

Strand Street.

Buitenkant Street.

The Castle.

Main Road, Woodstock.
Mosque, Long Street.

Schotsche Kloof.
Lutheran Church, Strand Street.

If one were to wander around Cape Town with an enquiring mind and inquisitive eye, the buildings of the city would tell of its history far more eloquently than any textbook could. For the architecture of Cape Town and its surrounds is interwoven with the history of the people who have lived here, from the founding settlement of the Dutch through to the present. During the period of Dutch tenure, which lasted more or less from the mid-seventeenth century until the close of the 1700s, French and other Europeans settled at the Cape. In fact, for a time they were actively encouraged to do so by Dutch authorities keen to bolster their fledgling colony against the possibility of British domination. Artisans were especially welcome. The Malay community, too, was established during this time and many of these immigrants from the East were also artisans. At the zenith of the Dutch East India Company fine buildings – homes as well as places of government, commerce and worship – came to grace the growing city, many owing their design and detail to the genius of Louis Michel Thibault, a Frenchman, and the German sculptor, Anton Anreith. But by the early nineteenth century the British were here to stay and the style of architecture changed completely: Regency, Georgian, Victorian and Edwardian.

Tamboerskloof.

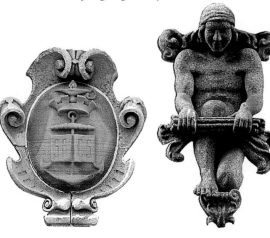

Jan Hendrik ('Onze Jan') Hofmeyr, scholar and politician.

Jan Smuts.   Queen Victoria.   Cecil John Rhodes.   Sir George Grey.

War memorial, Gardens.

General Louis Botha.

Bartholomeu Dias.

It is said that the writing of history is the prerogative of the victor, and certainly the statuary of Cape Town lends credence to this view, for the city abounds with the bronze and stone images of past notables. Bartholomeu Dias and Jan van Riebeeck are there, as are Jan Smuts and Louis Botha who, although both defeated Boer generals, regained their status and more as early prime ministers of the Union of South Africa. Queen Victoria, too, is there, still gazing out over one of the many dominions she ruled but never saw. One of her greatest champions was Cecil John Rhodes, arch imperialist, business tycoon and politician. He was a man of huge ambition and vision who dreamt of an Anglo-Africa reaching from Cape to Cairo. His influence, whether for good or bad, on the affairs of southern Africa was immense, but in 1902 he died dishonoured after an abortive attempt to seize control of the Transvaal Republic.

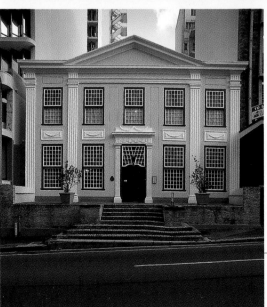

Koopmans-De Wet House has a history reaching back to the beginning of the eighteenth century, when it was built by one Reynier Smedinga, goldsmith and joint assayer to the Dutch East India Company. It subsequently passed through many hands and many alterations, gaining its present façade and proportions at the hands of the redoubtable team of Thibault and Anreith. In the early 1800s the house was bought by the De Wet family, in whose hands it remained until 1911. In the latter part of the nineteenth century it was occupied by Maria, a daughter of the family who had married Johan Koopmans in 1864. When Maria was widowed she and her sister continued to live at the Strand Street residence, directing their considerable energies into assembling a fine collection of period furniture. Today the house is a museum and well worth a visit, for it is redolent of the past century when it became a crossroads for the rich and famous of the time – dignitaries such as Cecil Rhodes and Paul Kruger were among those graciously received by the De Wet sisters.

Longmarket Street.

St George's Street.

There was a time when Cape Town was a far more 'lived in' city, especially in the days before District Six was demolished and its people summarily moved out at the instruction of the architects of apartheid. Overcrowded and a slum District Six might have been, but it was a vibrant, colourful and integral part of Cape Town, which has been much the poorer for its passing. In recent decades people have also been drawn out of the city by the strong movement of businesses to the suburbs, where huge shopping centres further reduce reliance on the city centre for many Capetonians. Of course people are still very much part of the city, but mostly as commuters moving daily to and from their places of work by car, bus, taxi and train. Planners are earnestly trying to win back popularity for the city centre, however, and with considerable success, particularly where streets have been closed to motor traffic and transformed into attractive pedestrian malls. Also, historic inner city residential areas, such as around Loader Street (opposite, third row, left), are being rediscovered and restored in period style. Happily, the tide is turning – Capetonians are coming back into their city.

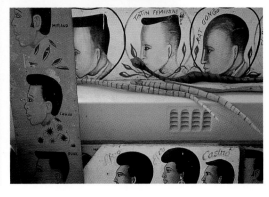

Although Cape Town's suburbs are no longer pierced by the braying tones of the fish horn announcing the presence of an itinerant fishmonger, food from the sea is still sold throughout the Peninsula from carts, the backs of 'bakkies' (open vans) and street corners, especially when the much-prized snoek are running. In fact, there is not much that you cannot buy off the street in Cape Town, where the trade of hawking is as old as the city itself. Today, the so-called 'informal sector' represents a substantial proportion of the local economy and provides a livelihood for thousands of Capetonians. Without it not only would they be materially worse off, but the city would be the poorer too. Cape Town would simply not be Cape Town without such long-established marketplaces as the Grand Parade where a deal can always be struck, whether over a bunch of dried traditional 'muti' herbs (bottom left), a bolt of brightly coloured fabric, a box of peaches, or a gold watch. The lively and often humorous banter between bargain-offering trader and sceptical customer, although all but incomprehensible to non-Capetonians, is an entertainment in itself. In more recent years the creation of pedestrian malls such as St George's Street (top left) has provided additional, and sometimes contentious, venues for the street traders.

Night falls over the city and a row of minibus taxis.

During the height of summer the sun sinks behind the mountains with seeming reluctance, leaving a lingering twilight to lengthen the evenings. But in winter it drops with almost indecent haste and city workers unable to make a quick getaway are likely to be finding their way home in the dark. For many, especially those who live far out in the townships and shanty towns that sprawl across the Cape Flats, the ride home will be in one of the minibus taxis lined up here as if for the start of Le Mans. As it happens, the analogy is not far from reality, for the taxi drivers are fiercely competitive and no quarter is given either to their colleagues on the road or to any other motorist. The general objective is to pack as many people as possible into their vehicles and then to deliver them to their destination at the highest speed the straining motors can muster. Accidents do happen, some of them horrific, but considering the velocity of these projectiles and the cavalier disregard for the highway code shown by their pilots, it is a matter of some wonder that there are not more.

Cape Town's flea-market culture extends far beyond the Grand Parade, its original venue, and these days stall-holders gather gypsy-like at various sites throughout the Peninsula. Almost every suburb has its own regular Saturday or Sunday market and the range of goods on offer is prodigious: leatherware, hand-made clothes, pottery, antique bottles, stamps, brassware, general bric-à-brac . . . The most famous of the flea markets is probably that held daily on Greenmarket Square in the city itself. The leafy square, with its cobbled streets and perimeter of handsome buildings – including the

Old Town House with its baroque façade and an art deco hotel – is a gathering place for locals and visitors alike. The market is an enthusiastic crush of tightly packed stalls and brightly coloured umbrellas. And always there is music to add to the general hubbub: marimba, jazz and the classics. Capetonians have always enjoyed their small speciality shops and the markets with their general informality. A few years ago expressions of spontaneity such as those shown on Greenmarket Square were frowned on by the city fathers, but now the 'move along' mentality is relaxing.

Aspects of the Tuynhuis: colonial verandah . . .

. . . the formal gardens . . .

. . . pediment detail.

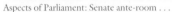
Aspects of Parliament: Senate ante-room . . .

. . . the Library of Parliament . . .

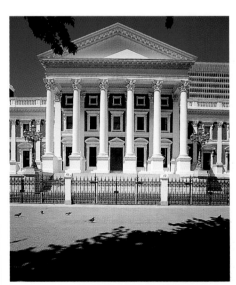
. . . the view from Government Avenue.

Few people, Capetonians included, have any idea of what lies beyond the guarded entrance to the Tuynhuis at the bottom of Roeland Street. Certainly there is no hint of the beautifully laid out formal gardens to the rear of the building that now houses the State President's Office. The security is understandable, but it is a pity that so few people may see this magnificent structure, which was built at the end of the seventeenth century as the guest house of the Dutch East India Company. Next door, the Houses of Parliament are of a much later vintage, for they were officially opened only in 1884. Later, at the time of Union, a new wing was brought into use to accommodate the House of Assembly. The Houses of Parliament have witnessed the full gamut of South Africa's modern history, including changes that for a time seemed impossible: transition from the deliberate creation of a land divided on the basis of skin colour to the recent process of healing. The imposing pile of Victorian and Edwardian opulence, once a symbol of prejudice and intolerance, now presides as a symbol of hope for the future of the country.

The ubiquitous grey squirrel
– an engaging immigrant
from Europe.

The area around the Houses of Parliament and other stately buildings that grace the city above Adderley Street is known simply as the Gardens. Bisected by Government Avenue which is flanked and canopied by venerable oaks, the Gardens are a little corner of tranquillity, a much-needed 'green lung' for the city. They are a place to stroll, or to sit and have lunch, a place to feed squirrels or simply to watch the world go by. Although steeped in history, the Gardens are very much a part of Cape Town today and it is, perhaps, a little difficult to imagine them in the role for which they were originally intended. The raison d'être *for the early Dutch*

The upper storey balcony of the Tuynhuis.

settlement was as a replenishment station for the merchantmen of the Dutch
East India Company. It was with some urgency, therefore, that planting began, but
the soils and the Cape climate were not kind and first attempts at cultivation met
with little success. But in time, and under the supervision of the appropriately named
Hendrik Boom, the Company Gardens began to take shape. For a while they
served their purpose, but soon agriculture took on the guise of free enterprise as
favoured company servants, Hendrik Boom among them, were released from their
company contracts to begin farming for themselves. With this process the focus of the
original Gardens progressed from market garden to a collection of botanical
specimens and, finally, to a place of recreation for the growing city.

Great Synagogue, Gardens.

Mosque, Dorp Street.

Groote Kerk, Adderley Street.

Religion being so often a divisive element in the world, it is perhaps surprising that in a country where social and political history has dwelt on the differences between people, the expression of worship has never led to the terrible conflicts experienced in other parts of the world. There are fundamental differences, of course, but by and large tolerance prevails and Christianity, Judaism and Islam, three of the world's greatest faiths, have played a huge role in the shaping of Cape Town. Churches, synagogues and mosques abound, many of them beautiful and fitting tributes not only to the Almighty, but also to the architectural genius of those who built them. Adding to the pervading calm of the Gardens is the Great Synagogue, its elegant baroque-style twin towers rising majestically above the trees. The synagogue was consecrated in 1905, but it was not the first place of worship for the colony's Jewry, for alongside is the Old Synagogue which was built in the Egyptian style in 1863 and is now the Jewish Museum. Not far from the Great Synagogue, at the city end of the Gardens, is the Groote Kerk. The church, built by Hermann Schutte, sometimes contractor to Thibault, is a somewhat strange marriage of Gothic, Egyptian and classical elements. It was dedicated in 1841, but the adjacent baroque clock tower, the only remaining part of the original church building on the site, dates from the beginning of the 1700s.

Lutheran Church and mosque,
Loop Street.

Moravian Chapel, District Six.

Muslim worshippers, District Six.

Looking down Long Street.

Long Street has to be the most photographed thoroughfare of the city, for more than any other it manifests the extraordinary amalgamation of cultures that have made Cape Town. At its lower end, where it joins the Foreshore, its character has been destroyed by irresponsible development, but as it journeys uphill towards the mountain it comes alive with churches, mosques, shops and hostelries representing and combining the whole gamut of period and style that has dictated Cape Town's architectural heritage. Overall, however, it is Victorian in character, with art nouveau and art deco detail and with cast-iron railings and 'brockie lace' decorating the balconies and verandahs. Among the most notable buildings are the Blue Lodge (below left), originally a rooming house and now Cape Town's only remaining example of a High Victorian corner building; the Palm Tree Mosque (above right, centre); the Green Hansom Hotel; the YMCA; and, undoubtedly one of Cape Town's loveliest architectural memorials, the Sendinggestig (Mission Foundation).

Fish cart, Salt River.

Although Cape Town, like any other large city, has its share of sprawling shopping centres with their
fashionable boutiques and obligatory supermarkets, the age of the high-street trader hangs on stubbornly.
From the Grand Parade and the city all the way to Muizenberg and beyond, the Main Road which threads its way
southwards through the suburbs is lined with independent merchants: the old-fashioned barber shop,
a tobacconist's kiosk, a pawnbroker, or an antique dealer. Fish is sold fresh from
the sea, cleaned and dressed to order, while fruit and vegetables
are sold at markets and at street corners,

Fruit and vegetable stall, central Cape Town.

weighed out straight from the box or basket – you are unlikely to find sophisticated supermarket packaging here! One of the more famous of the fresh food markets is that at Salt River, where the tiered and colourful displays of local produce are inviting. Depending on the season, this would also be the place to find those real Cape specialities such as sour figs and 'waterblommetjies'.

1 & 2 New Year – carnival time.

1
2

New Year is a special time in Cape Town: not only is it the height of the holiday season when beaches seethe with bodies and applause spatters out over the grandstands of Newlands Cricket Ground, but it is also the time of the 'Coon Carnival'. The carnival, which centres around a number of Mardi Gras-style rallies and processions, was originally a celebration of the New Year among the Cape's slave community, but after slavery was abolished in the early nineteenth century the tradition lived on and grew to be an exuberant and highly colourful street spectacle, much enjoyed by the participants as well as the crowds that lined the routes to watch. After months of hard preparation the troupes of banjo- and guitar-playing minstrels in their boaters and bright silks would come pouring out of District Six and elsewhere – until the 1970s when, destructive officialdom reigning supreme, they were told that this would no longer be allowed. Today the carnival is largely confined to a few stadiums, but hopefully its cheerful sounds will soon ring once more through the city streets at New Year.

3 & 4 Flower sellers off Adderley Street.

*Another quintessential aspect of Cape Town life is the tradition of the
flower seller. It would be hard to imagine a Cape Town without this doughty breed
of women and men who are all but impossible to ignore when they decide, with all
good humour, that you will buy their carnations, roses, glads . . .*

Preparing sweet-smelling sachets for the celebration of the Prophet's birthday is the prerogative of female members of the Muslim community.

Cape Town today has a significant Muslim community – the Cape Malays. But, as one commentator has observed, Islam did not come to the Cape as an already established way of life; instead, it grew into one with time. The reason behind the statement is that for the most part the forebears of the Cape Malays were brought to this country in the seventeenth and eighteenth centuries as slaves, not from Malaysia as their name would suggest, but from the Indonesian Archipelago – islands such as Bali, Timor, Buton, Java and the Celebes – an area that had only just begun to absorb Islam. (Recent authorities state that significant numbers of Muslims were also brought to the Cape from India and other parts of Africa.) At the time that the slaves arrived – there were four main influxes from the 1660s through to the mid-1700s – the young colony was woefully short of skilled labour and it was an opportunity for the Indonesians to carve a niche for themselves. Although many came from rural

The traditions of the community are passed from one generation to the next.

backgrounds, they quickly adapted to life in a town and soon had formed a sophisticated community plying trades from carpentry and masonry through to tailoring and shoemaking. Some, on payment of a fee to their owners, were permitted to live and work independently. Such freedom enabled them to hold religious meetings in their homes and these, together with their common language of Malayu, kept the slaves in contact with one another, leading to a strong bond and the growth of a Muslim culture which attracted non-Muslims as well. The practice of holding services kept the community together during a period of some 150 years when public expression of any religion other than that of the Dutch was forbidden. But the focus of Muslim life is the mosque, and after the community had petitioned long and hard to build one, permission was finally granted in 1807. Today there are few areas in the Peninsula that are beyond earshot of a muezzin calling the faithful to prayer.

Rose Street, Bokaap.

Al-Azhar – or Aspeling Street – Mosque, District Six.

Not all the early Indonesians at the Cape were slaves, for the colony was also used as a convict station and as a place of exile for high-ranking dissidents from the Dutch possessions in the East. The most famous of these was Sheikh Yusuf, a man of noble rank related to the kings of Goa and to one of the sultans of the Celebes. Much feared by the Dutch, he was sent into exile at the Cape at the age of 68. He died in 1699 and was buried some 20 kilometres from Cape Town. In the five years he spent here he gave enduring purpose and direction to the Muslim community, and to this day his kramat, or tomb, is regarded as a 'holy place'. Another leader who played a huge role in establishing Islam at the Cape was Tuan Guru. Of royal blood and an intellectual schooled in all aspects of the religion, he came to Africa in his middle age. He wrote prolifically and two of his most noted achievements

Kramat on Signal Hill, one of several around Cape Town.

Schotsche Kloof.

during his sojourn here were his book on Islamic jurisprudence and his having written out the Qur'an from memory when he found that no copy existed here at the time. He also organized the first school for Cape Muslims in the Bokaap where he lived, died and is buried. Although the impact of the Islamic faith is largely contained within the Muslim community, the broader aspects of their Indonesian culture has had a considerable influence on life at the Cape. For instance, many Malayu words were absorbed into the Dutch spoken locally and today they are very much part of the Dutch-derived Afrikaans language. But it is in matters of food that the impact has been arguably the greatest, for the dishes and delicacies that were brought from the East have given rise to a unique culinary tradition known as 'Cape Malay'.

Towards Mouille Point from the Sea Point Pavilion and, below, Sea Point with Table Mountain rising above the saddle between Signal Hill and Lion's Head.

On the other side of Signal Hill from the Bokaap lies a very different
Cape Town. Here, instead of the low, simple buildings in the styles of the past, tall
apartment blocks line the coast in a manner more reminiscent of Rio de Janeiro
and Hong Kong than the leisurely atmosphere usually associated with Cape Town.
There is little of architectural merit in the untidy jostle for command of the
best views out over the ocean and some parts of the suburb, set back from the front
rank, are somewhat run-down. There is a vibrancy about the area, however,
and at one time Sea Point was the undisputed epicentre of Cape Town
nightlife. In its heyday there were probably more restaurants here than in the rest
of the city put together, but although a number remain, the allegiance of
Capetonians and visitors alike is rapidly switching to the Waterfront development
a few kilometres down the coast.

Mouille Point during a winter gale.

An infrequent electrical storm over Table Bay.

Sea Point promenade is a regular venue for daily exercise . . .

. . . or a late-afternoon stroll.

Kelp gull.

Winter storms in Cape Town can be frightening, for they lash the
Peninsula with a terrible ferocity and can cause considerable damage.
Table Bay and its adjacent seaboard are particularly vulnerable to the
squalls that sweep in from the west. A winter anchorage in Table Bay was particularly
feared by early mariners and with just cause, for in those early days there was no safe haven.
No fewer than 300 ships were lost in Table Bay during the first 120 years of the settlement.
Even today the fury of the Northwester regularly claims its victims. However, when the sun
shines, as it does on most days, Sea Point promenade is a hive of activity.

Looking out from Signal Hill over Mouille Point and Green Point towards Robben Island.

Robben Island's jackass penguins.

View to Table Mountain.

Island church, built in 1841.

Victorian cottages.

Swift tern.

Robben Island lies in Table Bay about 10 kilometres across from the Mouille Point lighthouse. It is a low, windswept and uninviting place, made even more so by its long association with human misery and hardship. Almost continuously from the time that western man set foot on its shores to exploit its seals, its seabirds for their eggs and its stone for building, it has served as a penal settlement, leper colony, lunatic asylum and prison. More recently its notoriety has centred around the fact that South Africa's president, Nelson Mandela, and many of his colleagues were held on the island for so long as political prisoners. The future of Robben Island is uncertain, but many would like to see it as a monument and as a properly proclaimed nature conservation area. It appears, however, that the island's woes are not yet over, for conservation of its wildlife suffered a major setback in 1994 when a huge oilspill caused untold damage to the marine life and decimated the resident colony of jackass penguins.

A Clifton mansion, Victoria Road.

Clifton and its famous beaches.

Once St Gabriel's Church, now a home.

The road running southwards from rapidly out of the high-rise tumble round the rocky headland of Bantry ferent world – if Sea Point is South Sea Point, Victoria Road, climbs of hotels and apartment blocks to Bay. In doing so it enters a very dif- Africa's Copacabana, then Clifton is its Côte d'Azur. Here Lion's Head rises steeply to its summit 669 metres above the sea, while below the road that snakes its way around the lower slopes the land drops almost precipitously to the Atlantic Ocean and the tiny crescents of white sand known rather prosaically as First, Second, Third and Fourth beaches. On a cold wintery day, wrapped up warmly and enveloped in the thunder of heavy seas, the beaches are a place for solitude and a slow walk. In summer, however, Clifton Bay transforms into a mecca for sun worshippers. Undeterred by the surf that remains breath-robbingly cold throughout the year, they flock to the beaches to watch and be watched as their tans deepen. One of the great advantages of Clifton, aside from its unparalleled setting, is that it is one of the few places protected by a quirk of geography from the Southeaster, that notorious summer wind that can nag at the Peninsula for days.

Clifton homes clinging to the mountainside.

Clifton from the sea.

There is something about Clifton that suggests nouveau riche . . . Robin Leach's 'lifestyles of the rich and famous'. And the sense of Mediterranean playground, that combination of highly developed mountainside, white beaches and sparkling sea, is even stronger in summer when the cars of beachgoers make the narrow Victoria Road all but impassable, and motor cruisers and yachts crowd into Clifton Bay. For the most part the homes and apartments that cling tenaciously to the steep slopes above the beaches are expensive, very expensive, and a number are owned by European émigrés buying their place in the sun at very favourable exchange rates. Most of the houses and apartments are new and adventurous, their contemporary designs a test of engineering skill and the determination of owners to achieve that perfect view. For many the only access to their homes is via daunting flights of steps, but at least one homeowner has installed a funicular railway to provide an easy ride to his eyrie high on the flanks of Lion's Head.

Muizenberg beach.

The Cape Peninsula has a coastline of nearly 150 kilometres and for a good part of its length the peaks of the Table Mountain chain fall steeply into the sea. Here and there, however, the cliffs give way to a stretch of brilliant white sand. A few of these beaches – Noordhoek and Muizenberg for instance – curve lazily into the distance, while others such as Llandudno, Boulders and St James are little more than tucked-away coves. Some are great for bathing and some for the more adventurous sports of board-sailing and surfing, but all have their devotees and during Cape Town's long, hot, dry summer that extends from the end of October through to April, and sometimes even into May, many are invaded daily by those keen to soak up the sun. It is the balmy days of early autumn, however, that are often the best the Cape has to offer, a time when the days are still warm – the temperature regularly reaches into the high twenties – and the persistent Southeaster that can make a summer excursion to many beaches an unpleasant, gritty experience has usually tired itself to no more than a soft breeze.

70

Seaforth, near Simon's Town.

Clifton.

Llandudno.

Camps Bay and the Twelve Apostles.

Camps Bay beach scenes and, top left, The Bay Hotel.

The Round House, Camps Bay Glen.

The winding road through the Glen.

Indigenous pelargonium.

Camps Bay is one of Cape Town's most beautiful suburbs. Less ostentatious than Clifton, perhaps, it is nevertheless a refuge of the city's better-heeled citizens. Its setting is incomparable, with spacious homes and gardens below the soaring buttresses of the Twelve Apostles that together form the western face of the Table Mountain massif. Unfortunately much of Camps Bay regularly feels the full brunt of the summer Southeaster, but this does little to detract from the popularity of the suburb or its long, wide beach. The undoubted focus of entertainment in Camps Bay is The Bay Hotel; stylish and sophisticated, it caters for overseas visitors and a growing executive clientele eager for an alternative to staying in the city. In the adjacent shopping mall is the rather noisy, but hugely popular, Blues Restaurant. Those who prefer a less frenetic culinary experience patronize the Round House, in the lee of Lion's Head and once a nineteenth-century hunting lodge.

Bakoven from the air.

Llandudno.

At Camps Bay's southern extremity is the much smaller Bakoven Bay, so-named for the low, rounded rock that bulges out of the surf just offshore. Clearly visible in the wall of the domed boulder is a smoothly curved opening, the overall effect being remarkably like that of a bakoven, the Dutch word for a clay oven. The tight little community of cottages that cluster around Bakoven Bay marks the end of suburbia and for several kilometres Victoria Road winds free of development towards Llandudno.

Looking back towards Lion's Head and Camps Bay from Llandudno.

Cape cormorant.

Bakoven Bay.

From the road above the picturesque collection of mostly very beautiful homes that make up the exclusive hamlet of Llandudno, the view back from the lookout towards Lion's Head with Camps Bay at its feet is memorable, whether in brilliant summer sunshine or during the brooding depths of winter. It is also an excellent spot for a lesson in the geology of the Peninsula. Essentially, three types of rock make up the Table Mountain range: shales, here and there showing through on the lower slopes as reddish clay soils; Cape granite, very obvious as the rounded grey boulders on the lower slopes of Lion's Head and the Twelve Apostles right down to the shoreline; and Table Mountain Sandstone, a sedimentary rock laid down over the shales and granite. Some 250 million years ago huge buckling and uplifting of the sedimentary deposits gave rise to the mountains – time, wind and water have slowly sculpted them into the shapes we see today.

Hout Bay from the fishing harbour.

To early seafarers hugging the western flank of the Peninsula as they sailed to and from their anchorage in Table Bay, the deep haven a few sea miles down the coast that was guarded by cliffs dropping sheer into the sea must have soon become a familiar sight. It wasn't long before the bay was explored and its thickly wooded valley noted with interest. Indeed, it was called Houtbaai, literally Wood Bay, and has retained this name to the present. We know that soon after his arrival Jan van Riebeeck, first commander of the settlement, despatched a party to investigate the bay and its surrounds, and it was not long after that that the exploitation of the bay for its

Looking towards Hout Bay from Chapman's Peak.

timber began. As the settlement at the foot of Table Mountain grew, so did the demand for building timber. Soon the slopes of the mountain were cropped of their forest and resources farther afield, such as those at Hout Bay, were greedily attacked. It is probably only because the upper slopes of the valley were largely inaccessible that the forest survived to enjoy its present-day protected status. For much of the valley's history timber and farming were the major sources of revenue. Today Hout Bay is a burgeoning town with tourism and fishing as the centre of its economic life. Indeed, the two activities go hand in hand, for the busy life in the harbour is a perennial attraction to visitors.

Fishing boats, Hout Bay.

The harbour with its fleet of brightly painted fishing smacks lies on the northern flank of Hout Bay. Behind it tower the Sentinel and the Karbonkelberg to complete what must be one of the most photographed scenes in all of South Africa. Quaint as it may appear, however, the harbour is a busy place, for it is the headquarters of the local crayfishing industry as well as other important fisheries. Synonymous with Hout Bay is snoek – a voracious predatory fish that is a highly regarded local delicacy – and during the season the incoming boats are eagerly met by those impatient to buy their evening meal straight from the dockside.

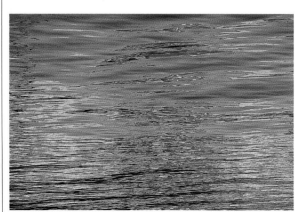

A good haul of snoek.

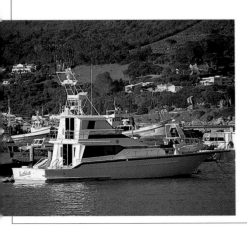

With a history going back almost as far  as that of Cape Town, Hout Bay is in a sense a microcosm of the city, sharing similar opportunities and problems. Cape Town bears the dubious honour of being one of the fastest growing cities in the world, and certainly many of Hout Bay's residents feel that their share of the experience is rather discomforting. Yet the casual visitor may find this difficult to believe, for the bayside and adjacent valley have an idyllic quality, and this is enhanced by the undeniably spectacular setting. The village and lovely beach impart an air of permanent holiday, a laid-back atmosphere that is very seductive. Indeed, it is these qualities that have made Hout Bay a very desirable place to live in. However, problems lie just below the surface; it is held that the rapid expansion of Hout Bay through ill-considered housing developments, together with a growing informal 'squatter' settlement and an inadequate sewage system, are seriously compromising the suburb's ability to realize the full potential of a long-term sustainable way of life based on its thriving tourism and fishing industries.

1 Surfing at Kommetjie.
2 Southern right whale.
3 Chapman's Peak Drive.

The gradient of the coastal road as it leaves Hout Bay on its way towards Noordhoek is impressive to say the least. It marks the start of Chapman's Peak Drive, a tortuous route that was literally carved out of the mountainside by Italian prisoners held in South Africa during the Second World War. Rising and falling, twisting and turning, the road follows the fault line between the layer of granite, which drops away – in places some 200 metres – to the surging tides below, and the Table Mountain Sandstone, which reaches to the peaks of Constantiaberg, Noordhoek and Chapman's itself. The views of mountain and crashing seas are breathtaking, and the drive is considered to be among the most spectacular scenic routes in the world.

Kommetjie.

The waters along the western coast of the Cape Peninsula are without exception cold, and even in summer not many swimmers are prepared to numb body and soul. Some of the best surfing and crayfishing spots are along this coast, however, and it is a common sight to see wetsuited figures skimming down the face of a wave or bobbing about next to a fishing boat just behind the surf line. It is not unusual, either, to suddenly become aware of the long dark shape of a southern right whale rolling lazily in the swell or to see a massive, fluked tail flick at the air, the only hint of the huge mammal below the surface.

Noordhoek beach, with Kommetjie and the Slangkop lighthouse in the far distance.

Seashore life of the Cape coast.

Noordhoek beach, that long stretch of uninterrupted white sand between the cliffs below Chapman's Peak Drive and far-off Kommetjie, is one of the loneliest spots on the entire Peninsula. Its inviting but treacherous waters make swimming inadvisable and the reputation of quicksands adds a sense of lurking danger, an almost primal quality, to the landscape. Early man lived in these parts, as we know from findings in nearby Peer's Cave, above Fish Hoek, that date back 25 000 years, and it is not difficult to imagine our Stone Age ancestors as part of the setting. Any such reverie is

Chacma baboons.

quickly dispelled, however, on casting one's eyes inland. The beach marks the western limit of the Noordhoek Valley which extends through to the town of Fish Hoek on the False Bay coast. Here the scene is very different from the one that would have confronted Fish Hoek Man, for the valley, which incorporates valuable wetlands, is rapidly being transformed by suburban housing developments and informal settlements, while the indigenous vegetation is being seriously threatened by invading alien plants.

Smitswinkel Bay, from the Cape of Good Hope Nature Reserve.

Wreck of the *Thomas Tucker*.

Wreck of the *Nolloth*.

Smitswinkel Bay.

Spindrift near Cape Point.

Every year more than 400 000 people visit the Cape of Good Hope Nature Reserve, one of the most important botanical conservation areas on the Peninsula. Few stop, however, to explore the wonder of the fynbos vegetation as they hasten across the windswept plateau, impatient to reach Cape Point and the legendary meeting place of the Atlantic and Indian oceans. Whether they do meet here or whether the honour belongs to Cape Agulhas to the east is academic, but there is no argument that the turbulent seas off this tumble of granite rocks mark the divide between the icy waters of the Peninsula's western coast and the comparatively warmer waters of False Bay on its eastern flank.

St George's Street, Simon's Town.

A quiet stroll along St George's Street, the main road of Simon's Town, reveals a quaint little village where time appears to have stopped at the turn of the century. There are obvious reminders of the present, of course, but an active and largely successful historical and conservation movement among residents and others has done much to ensure the survival of Simon's Town's architectural heritage. Among the many buildings of note are Admiralty House, the Residency – which after many years as a magistrates' court has been restored to house the Simon's Town Museum – and the Martello Tower, built in 1796 and now the Naval Museum.

Looking up to the mountain from Jubilee Square.

Simon's Town, headquarters of the South African fleet.

Simon's Town and the bay on which it stands take their name from Simon van der Stel, an enterprising administrator who came to the Cape in 1679 as commander, and later governor, of the small settlement. He surveyed the bay in 1687 and recommended that it be used as a winter anchorage, a refuge from the fierce northwesterly storms that were proving such a hazard to shipping in Table Bay. In 1814 Simon's Town became the South Atlantic base for the Royal Navy and remained as such until 1957, when it was handed over to the South African Navy. Of the copious stories, both fact and fiction, that are associated with the town, none is perhaps as endearing as that of 'Able Seaman Just Nuisance', the Great Dane which befriended sailors during the Second World War. A statue to this extraordinary dog stands in Jubilee Square.

1 & 2 Kalk Bay harbour under siege from a gale-force Southeaster.

It was only later that the southern tip of the African continent became known as the Cape of Good Hope – to the first Portuguese explorers of the late fifteenth century it was the Cape of Storms. And when the full might of a summer Southeaster or a winter Northwester unleashes itself on the Cape coast, it is not hard to sympathize with those early mariners in their puny sailing ships. Most coastal cities of the world are windy places – it is in the nature of an interface between land and sea – but Cape Town seems to have won particular notoriety. In the winter months low pressure systems move in off the southern oceans, hitting the Peninsula as wave after wave of cold fronts that bring rain, sometimes hard and driven and sometimes

The sea at Camps Bay flattened by an offshore Southeaster.

little more than a gentle drizzle. This westerly movement continues throughout the year, although in summer cooling in the northern hemisphere forces these systems further towards the Antarctic and they pass well to the south of the country. It is during these warmer months that the weather pattern is dominated by the strong South Atlantic high pressure system, bringing with it the mostly dry Southeaster. Along the western Cape's coastline, where there is an abundance of rocky headlands and mountains rising close to the sea, the wind speed is increased. For instance, at Cape Point it may reach gale force almost every day during the summer months.

89

1 & 2 Kalk Bay harbour.

On the False Bay coast northwards from Simon's Town through to Muizenberg a number of hamlets, villages and towns line the scenic rail route running just above the high water mark. Of them, the adjacent settlements of Kalk Bay with its tiny fishing harbour and St James with its postage-stamp beach lined with gaily painted bathing booths are the prettiest. St James is one of the few coves along this stretch of coast that is protected from the Southeaster.

Bathing booths and the beach at St James.

2

Kalk Bay derives its name from the Dutch word kalk, *meaning lime, an allusion to the shells that were burnt to produce the main ingredient of the whitewash used for painting buildings. Fishing, however, has been the more enduring activity of Kalk Bay and the suitability of its natural harbour for this pursuit was noted as early as Simon van der Stel's explorations of the area in the late 1600s. Subsequently it became an important whaling station, but this industry fell on hard times in the early years of the nineteenth century and gradually a more glamorous era for the village began as a 'salubrious and fashionable watering hole – the Brighton of the Cape' according to commentary in the* Cape Monitor.

Muizenberg beach.

Like Kalk Bay and St James, the town of Muizenberg, neatly arranged along the lower slopes of the mountain of the same name, was a fashionable seaside resort during the later years of Queen Victoria's reign and on into the early part of the new century. It was one of Rudyard Kipling's favourite places and his enthusiasm for the town and its beautiful, wide beach was shared by, among many others, Cecil Rhodes. After the humiliating events leading up to the Anglo-Boer War, Rhodes retired to his home on the Main Road and died there soon afterwards. Rhodes' Cottage, as it is now known, is maintained as a museum and contains many of the extraordinary man's personal possessions. It is one of a number of buildings of historical and

architectural importance in the town; others include the Posthuys which is believed to have been completed in 1673, a year before the Cape Town castle, as well as Sandhills, Rust en Vrede and Vergenoeg (top right) which all bear the gracious stamp of Sir Herbert Baker's prolific genius. Muizenberg still shows some of its Victorian and Edwardian charm – in its quaint Victorian station, for example, with its clock tower (top left) – but, no longer in vogue, it now has an air of being simply 'old-fashioned'. In recent years attempts have been made to inject new life into the town, the elaborate pavilion being an example, but essentially Muizenberg is a sleepy resort that wakens each year for a few months of holiday activity, then subsides once more into an extended winter hibernation.

Sunrise over Muizenberg beach.

Muizenberg beach – the view towards St James.

On a clear, still morning with the sun rising over the distant Hottentots Holland mountains, Muizenberg beach is an incomparable setting. One of the safest and most popular bathing spots in all the Peninsula, its white sands slope gradually to the water's edge and continue eastwards as far as the eye can see; but for the rocky intrusion from far-off Wolfgat to Swartklip, they extend without interruption clear across False Bay to the towns of Strand and Gordon's Bay. False Bay derives its name from the fact that early navigators returning from the East often mistakenly assumed Cape Hangklip, the massive headland at the eastern limit of the bay, to be Cape Point. As they discovered, they had not rounded the Cape to enter Table Bay and hence the appellation, False Bay.

Skeleton Gorge on the eastern face of Table Mountain.

The front face of Table Mountain is bare and formidable, a continuous grey wall reaching to the apparently flat summit that gives the mountain its name. There are easy ascents such as the long slog up Platteklip Gorge, but many more are a testing challenge of the rock-climber's skills. It is a serious mistake to underestimate the mountain; it can be unforgiving, and is especially treacherous in high winds and when thick clouds descend to turn bright daylight into a misty, disorienting gloom within a few frightening minutes. The least strenuous

In Newlands Forest.

The upper cableway station.

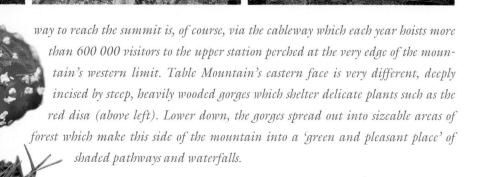

way to reach the summit is, of course, via the cableway which each year hoists more than 600 000 visitors to the upper station perched at the very edge of the mountain's western limit. Table Mountain's eastern face is very different, deeply incised by steep, heavily wooded gorges which shelter delicate plants such as the red disa (above left). Lower down, the gorges spread out into sizeable areas of forest which make this side of the mountain into a 'green and pleasant place' of shaded pathways and waterfalls.

Pine plantation in Cecilia State Forest.

Riding in Constantia.

Erica.

For the people who live in Cape Town's leafy southern suburbs the mountain is literally their back garden and there is a sense of camaraderie among those taking their leisure on its slopes. It is a favourite place for wandering with a dog, riding along one of the many bridle paths, or testing one's fitness over an arduous jogging route. Many Capetonians consider it a pity that not all the wooded areas are treed with indigenous species but, one's environmental conscience aside, the plantations of pines and blue gums also have a charm. Nor are their healthy populations of grey squirrels any less appealing for having being introduced via Europe from their original home in North America.

Newlands Forest.

The eastern face of the Table Mountain massif.

Little Chelsea, Wynberg.

If the wealth of the homeowners along Cape Town's Atlantic seaboard manifests itself rather obviously, then the opposite is true in the southern suburbs that are ranged under the shadow of Table Mountain's eastern flank. In many parts – Constantia, Kenilworth, Bishopscourt, Wynberg Hill and Newlands, for example – the homes are no less opulent, but they stand discreetly behind tall hedges and at the end of long, treed driveways. Even where the homes are more modest, clustered in Wynberg's Little Chelsea or lining some of the suburbs' major streets, the lifestyle is altogether less frenetic than it is in the Atlantic suburbs. Everywhere the forest-clad mountain looms as a backdrop, lending a sense of space which is enhanced by public parks and gardens.

Wedding scenes in Claremont Gardens and Wynberg Park.

Newlands homes.

Path to Skeleton Gorge.

Featherheads.   Silver tree.   Agapanthus.   'Blou suikerbos' protea.   Erica.

Camphor tree avenue.

Aloe garden.

Lesser doublecollared sunbird.

Sprawling beneath the majestic buttress known as Castle Rock (above right) is Kirstenbosch, the loveliest public garden of all and, indeed, one of the greatest in the world. Only southern African plants are represented in the garden, making its extensive collection unique. The focus, however, is on the Cape flora which, although covering only four per cent of South Africa's land surface, comprises about 8 500 species and is regarded as constituting one of the six floral kingdoms of the world. The Kirstenbosch gardens are much loved by Capetonians and are on the itinerary of anyone passing through the city. Each day hundreds, if not thousands, of visitors pass through, but even before the gates open at eight o'clock, regulars may sneak in through a side entrance to enjoy the peace and solitude of an early jog or amble in the gardens. Even at weekends and on public holidays Kirstenbosch never seems crowded, and a short walk beyond the well-beaten circuit around the restaurant and shop will always be rewarded with a sense of having the place to oneself. Not only does the network of paths lead one through the collections of proteas, ericas, cycads, pelargoniums and other indigenous plants, but it also provides access to the mountain and two of the most popular ascents, up Nursery Ravine and Skeleton Gorge.

River lily.

Pincushion.

Red disa.

Suurkanol.

Gousblom.

Bitter aloe.

Sunshine protea.

Entrance to Klein Constantia.

Wine was made at the Cape not long after the Dutch first landed. It probably wasn't very good wine, but it was wine none the less – and so began a tradition of winemaking that has continued to the present. In recent years particularly, Cape wines have made great strides in their complexity and sophistication and have placed South Africa firmly on the map of winemaking nations of the world. As with so many aspects of Cape culture and early development, it was the colony's first governor, Simon van der Stel, who laid the foundation of the wine industry in South Africa. It was during his tenure that the town of Stellenbosch – considered to be the wine capital of the country – was founded; it was he who settled French Huguenots in the Franschhoek Valley which is also a focus of winemaking; and it was he who saw the potential of the Constantia Valley. In this beautiful, and to this day still remarkably rural, setting he established his huge estate of Groot Constantia.

The front gable, Groot Constantia.

Buitenverwachting Estate.

The old wine cellar, Groot Constantia, now part of the museum.

His attempts at viticulture were successful, and of particular note was his sweet wine in the character of those fashionable in Europe at the time. 'Constantia' became a household name, much appreciated locally and abroad. Wines continue to be made in the Constantia Valley, and although much reduced from its original extent, Groot Constantia is still a working wine farm with a vast modern cellar. After a devastating fire in 1925 the stately homestead was restored faithfully to the façade and additions made at the end of the eighteenth century. It is now a museum, while the out-buildings form a complex of restaurants, taverns and shops.

The homestead and vineyards of Buitenverwachting.

Constantia Valley landscape.

The old cellar, Buitenverwachting.

The wines of Groot Constantia are still well regarded, but during the 1980s and 1990s winemaking in the valley has undergone something of a renaissance with the farms of Klein Constantia and Buitenverwachting, both owing their origins to Van der Stel's original estate, producing Chardonnays, Sauvignon Blancs and Bordeaux-style reds to match the best the country has to offer. Klein Constantia has even produced a 'Vin de Constance', an outstanding recreation of the wines that made Constantia so famous in the eighteenth and nineteenth centuries. Not to be outdone, Buitenverwachting (the name means 'beyond expectation') has combined good winemaking with good food and boasts one of the finest and most exclusive restaurants in South Africa.

Front verandah, Groote Schuur.

One of Cape Town's grandest residences is Groote Schuur, another creation of Sir Herbert Baker, but not regarded among his best. The history of the estate, however, predates Baker by some 250 years, for Groote Schuur's original structure was indeed the 'great barn' suggested by its Dutch name and was part of Jan van Riebeeck's granary. It was to pass through many owners before eventually coming into the hands of Cecil John Rhodes, who commissioned the young Baker to create for him a mansion. After the fire which destroyed his original thatched restoration of Groote Schuur, Baker reconstructed the house with its familiar tall gables and 'barley sugar' chimneys.

Domestic staff, Herschel School for Girls.

Tabora Manor House, Newlands.

Fine wines, fine food, fine architecture and fine education would be a reasonable if somewhat simplistic summation of Cape Town's southern suburbs. In addition to Buitenverwachting, the Alphen Hotel, also with a history reaching back to the early settlement of the Constantia Valley, has a restaurant of note, as does the Constantia Uitsig farm. And although other eateries in the area may not enjoy quite the same rural settings, their standards remain high and many are housed in good old buildings. And when it comes to schools, such household names as 'Bishops', Herschel, Rondebosch, SACS, Westerford, Wynberg and Rustenberg roll off the tongue, a litany of South Africa's oldest and most revered educational institutions.

Alphen Hotel, Constantia.

The library, Hawthornden.

At the junction of Newlands and Tennant roads, where the suburbs of Claremont, Kenilworth and Wynberg meet, a winding lane twists dangerously across the main thoroughfare and continues off to the right. This is Herschel Walk which, like the famous school sited on its lower reaches, takes its name from Sir John Herschel, astronomer and amateur botanist who came to the Cape in the mid-1800s and did much to foster culture and education in the burgeoning British colony. An amble along Herschel Walk is a restful diversion, made even more pleasurable when one rounds a bend and is confronted by cast-iron railings and the elegant façade of Hawthornden set in a well-tended garden. It is a Victorian/ Edwardian residence in the grand style and although much of the building is hidden from

Hawthornden.

view, its western aspect is close to the road and open doors and windows sometimes provide tantalizing glimpses of the elegant interior. The original homestead on the site, De Oude Wynberg, was built in 1775 and the present house – commissioned by one Captain John Spence and making its appearance in 1882 – was based on its foundations. Later the property was purchased by the mining magnate Sir Joseph ('JB') Robinson who added further to the home. Yet again the hand of Sir Herbert Baker was involved, on this occasion in the refurbishment of the library. Hawthornden has remained in the Robinson family and is now owned by Sir Joseph's grandson, Count Natale Labia, whose renowned art collection (including a Van Dyck School portrait of Princess Mary, opposite page) hangs in the beautifully proportioned and appointed mansion.

The University of Cape Town with Devil's Peak rising behind.

Old graveyard adjacent to Groote Schuur Hospital.

Devil's Peak from the Black River.

Examination time.

Superlatives abound when one tries to do justice to the beauty of the Peninsula and the setting of its many famous landmarks, but even they are inadequate to describe the University of Cape Town, set into the slopes of Devil's Peak like some high monastic town. It owes its incomparable position to the vision of none other than Cecil John Rhodes whose spirit – his physical remains lie buried in the Matobo Hills of Zimbabwe – broods over his nearby memorial (right) which faces north, towards the empire from Cape to Cairo that never materialized. The university has a highly respected medical faculty whose students train at the nearby Groote Schuur Hospital.

Cape Town is nothing if not a city of contrasts: sea and mountain, rocky headlands and sandy beaches, bare cliff faces and thickly wooded kloofs, still, crystal-clear days and protracted nagging winds. But the contrasts don't all relate to topography, geology and climate – they are just as apparent in the lifestyles of the people who call themselves Capetonians. On a mountain-hugging trip around the Peninsula there are few interruptions to the flow of well-to-do living. But, as one nears completion of the circular tour and skirts the lower slopes of Devil's Peak to return towards the city, passing through Mowbray and entering the suburbs of Observatory, Woodstock and Salt River, it is a treeless, drab world that emerges. Along the Main Road, where buses, taxis and cars vie for pole position at traffic lights, shops of all sizes and trades crowd one another, from

bakeries to haberdashers and furnishers, from second-hand car lots to battery and tyre discounters. Off it, down narrow backstreets, grim tenements and terraces stand unpainted and unloved. Tired women scold urchins in the street and despair seems endemic. But it is not all like that, and even here contrast is the order of the day. Once, at the turn of the century, parts of these suburbs were well thought of and a hundred years on they are being rediscovered. Dilapidated Victorian cottages are being lovingly restored and a yuppy affluence is moving in. Restaurants, pubs and jazz venues thrive, and quaint little shops selling bric-à-brac and antiques lie tucked under verandahed walkways. And so, back from the bustling Main Road, there is a seedy vibrancy, an amalgam of past and present that make for a promising future for these inner city suburbs.

Much is made of Cape Town's past and there can be little argument that it is
the constant reminders of bygone eras that lend the city much of its charm.
But it is a modern city too, with its fair share of sophisticated hotel complexes
and shopping centres where wine shops, clothing boutiques, travel agents,
restaurants, hair salons and health shops rub shoulders along wide marbled
pedestrian malls. Cinemas, fast-food outlets and computer-game arcades are also
part of the scene, and if it were not for Cape Town's unique blend of languages
and cultures, the urbane face it wears today could be confused with that of almost
any other cosmopolitan city in the world.

Downtown Cape Town.

Long Street.

Lower Long Street.

Adderley Street.

St George's Street.

Cape Sun Hotel, Strand Street.

Thibault Square.   St George's Mall.

Cape Town, Mother City, the Tavern of the Seas, may be young compared with other cities of the world, but she is South Africa's grand old lady. The settlement's site beneath Table Mountain is an ancient one, the story of which will never really be known let alone recounted. And, from tenuous beginnings as a wood-and-mud fort and a scattering of unprepossessing dwellings, Cape Town has both witnessed the gamut of the country's social and political history, and played a seminal role in it. Today Capetonians are aware of their past, aware that aspects of it have left deep social wounds. But they are also aware of a heritage of which there is much to be proud. Most importantly of all, however, they are aware of the future and the promise and opportunity it holds. Cape Town has been nominated as Africa's bid for the Olympics of 2004, and the opportunity will be taken to use the event positively for the people of Cape Town and their environment. Now, at the threshold of the new millenium, there is a sense that the city is beginning to take charge of its destiny – environmental and social problems, of which there are many, are being faced imaginatively and with a determination that was seldom evident in the past.

From the wetland reserve of Rietvlei on the west coast north of Table Bay,
the view of Table Mountain and its companions Lion's Head and Devil's Peak is
probably little different from that gazed upon by human beings thousands upon thousands of years ago.
It is not hard, especially when a low mist hangs over the sea, to imagine that there is no city there
at all and, like the first European explorers who approached from the north in their tiny sailing ships,
one is seeing an island rising out of the sea . . . But there is a difference. Gone are the people
who gathered food from the sea and grazed their cattle on the plains, gone are the hippos that snorted in the
Liesbeeck River and the lions that once hunted in Table Valley, and gone is much of the
natural vegetation that evolved in concert with the climate, geology and animal life. The environment
of the Cape Peninsula has been irrevocably altered by the hand of man, and in times of
reflection it is difficult not to feel guilt at our presumption. On the other hand, our interference
has created Cape Town, one of the most beautiful and exciting cities in all the world.